June 2008

Blue Banner Biographies

Johnny Depp

Kathleen Tracy

Mitchell Lane
PUBLISHERS

P.O. Box 196
Hockessin, Delaware 19707
Visit us on the web: www.mitchelllane.com
Comments? email us: mitchelllane@mitchelllane.com

Mitchell Lane PUBLISHERS

Printing   2   3   4   5   6   7   8   9

Blue Banner Biographies

Akon	Alan Jackson	Alicia Keys
Allen Iverson	Ashanti	Ashlee Simpson
Ashton Kutcher	Avril Lavigne	Bernie Mac
Beyoncé	Bow Wow	Britney Spears
Carrie Underwood	Chris Brown	Chris Daughtry
Christina Aguilera	Christopher Paul Curtis	Ciara
Clay Aiken	Condoleezza Rice	Daniel Radcliffe
David Ortiz	Derek Jeter	Eminem
Eve	Fergie (Stacy Ferguson)	50 Cent
Gwen Stefani	Ice Cube	Jamie Foxx
Ja Rule	Jay-Z	Jennifer Lopez
Jessica Simpson	J. K. Rowling	**Johnny Depp**
JoJo	Justin Berfield	Justin Timberlake
Kate Hudson	Keith Urban	Kelly Clarkson
Kenny Chesney	Lance Armstrong	Lindsay Lohan
Mariah Carey	Mario	Mary J. Blige
Mary-Kate and Ashley Olsen	Michael Jackson	Miguel Tejada
Missy Elliott	Nancy Pelosi	Nelly
Orlando Bloom	P. Diddy	Paris Hilton
Peyton Manning	Queen Latifah	Ron Howard
Rudy Giuliani	Sally Field	Selena
Shakira	Shirley Temple	Tim McGraw
Usher	Zac Efron	

Library of Congress Cataloging-in-Publication Data
Tracy, Kathleen.
    Johnny Depp / by Kathleen Tracy.
        p. cm. — (Blue banner biographies)
    Includes bibliographical references and index.
    ISBN 978-1-58415-614-7 (library bound)
    1. Depp, Johnny—Juvenile literature. 2. Motion picture actors and actresses—United States—Biography—Juvenile literature. I. Title.
PN2287.D39T73 2008
791.4302′8092—dc22
[B]   2007019683

ABOUT THE AUTHOR: Kathleen Tracy has been a journalist for over twenty years. Her writing has been featured in magazines including *The Toronto Star*'s "Star Week," *A&E Biography* magazine, *KidScreen* and *TV Times*. She is also the author of numerous biographies, including *William Hewlett: Pioneer of the Computer Age* and *The Fall of the Berlin Wall, Gwen Stefani, Mariah Carey,* and *Kelly Clarkson* for Mitchell Lane Publishers.

PHOTO CREDITS: Cover—Gregg DeGuire/Getty Images; pp. 4, 28—Peter Mountain56/WALT DISNEY/The Kobal Collection/WireImage; pp. 7, 9, 25—Alpha/Globe Photos; p. 12—Frazer Harrison/Getty Images; p. 14—Barry King/WireImage; p. 16—Chris Gordon/Getty Images; p. 18—Tom Rodriguez/Globe Photos; p. 21—Zade Rosenthal_64/20th Century FOX/The Kobal Collection/WireImage; p. 22—Peter Iovino_41/Paramount/The Kobal Collection/WireImage; p. 23—Bruce Birmelin/MGM/The Kobal Collection/WireImage; p. 27—Bob Riha Jr./WireImage.

PUBLISHER'S NOTE: The following story has been thoroughly researched, and to the best of our knowledge represents a true story. While every possible effort has been made to ensure accuracy, the publisher will not assume liability for damages caused by inaccuracies in the data and makes no warranty on the accuracy of the information contained herein. This story has not been authorized or endorsed by Johnny Depp.

Blue Banner Biography

For most of his career, Johnny Depp was the ultimate Hollywood outsider, best known for playing quirky, off-beat characters. His eccentric portrayal of Captain Jack Sparrow has made him one of the world's biggest box office stars and helped turn Disney's **Pirates of the Caribbean** *movies into one of the most successful film franchises in Hollywood history.*

Captain Jack

*T*he Disney film executives were worried. Very worried. For the first time in the company's history, they were making a movie based on one of their theme park attractions. They had bet $140 million that *Pirates of the Caribbean: Curse of the Black Pearl* would be a success. And now, they weren't sure they'd be lucky enough to break even on their investment. Some doubted they'd even be able to release the film.

What had they been *thinking* to hire Johnny Depp in the first place? Sure, the executives reminded each other, he was a good actor; a great actor — maybe the best actor of his generation. And they had known he was a little . . . how to say this nicely . . . a little *eccentric*. Liked to do things his own way; liked to keep people guessing. But they never anticipated this. . . .

The *this* that was giving Disney executives an ulcer was Depp's inventive portrayal of Captain Jack Sparrow, the pirate hero of the movie. Depp had shown up on the first day of filming with all his front teeth covered in gold caps, turning his movie star smile into scrap metal. After he refused to lose the gold, the executives compromised and let him keep all but two of the teeth capped.

The next problem was his performance. Pirates were supposed to be swashbuckling and brave, rough and tumble—which, in fact, Depp's Sparrow was, in his own way. But Captain Jack was also flamboyant and spacey and, well, a little too feminine at times for the executives' comfort. This was supposed to be a family film, after all, and they fretted some more.

> He recalled . . . how he finally "sat down with [Disney executives] and said, 'You hired me to do my job. If you can't trust me, you've got to replace me.' "

Depp told David Letterman the executives finally expressed their concern "with frantic phone calls. They called and said they didn't know what I was doing, exactly, with the character. They were concerned that I was, I think their words were, *ruining the movie.*

"Basically, what it got down to was, what is Captain Jack doing? 'We can't understand a word he's saying. Is he drunk? Are *you* drunk? Is he gay?' And of course, 'Are *you* gay?' "

Depp laughed at the memory, saying the point was not to do the same old portrayal of a pirate. "I wanted to avoid the parrot on my shoulder thing."

He recalled in *People* how he finally "sat down with [Disney executives] and said, 'You hired me to do my job. If you can't trust me, you've got to replace me.' "

They blinked and backed off, but the movie's producer, Jerry Bruckheimer, admitted to *Newsweek,* "It took a little while to calm everybody down." Director Gore Verbinski seemed amused by the flap. "You know, there's a lot of

Although he may seem confident onscreen, for much of his career, Depp struggled with being famous. He once admitted, "I'm shy, paranoid, whatever word you want to use. I hate fame. I've done everything I can to avoid it."

conspiring that goes on between actors and directors that I think is very healthy. You should be a little concerned as a director if you're *not* making the studio nervous."

Depp later admitted that the inspiration for Captain Jack was a combination of Rolling Stones guitarist Keith Richards and the romantic French cartoon skunk Pepé Le Pew.

> *"I thought pirates were sort of the rock 'n roll stars and Keith [Richards] has always been a great hero to me. He's the king of all rock stars."*

"I thought pirates . . . were sort of the rock 'n roll stars and Keith has always been a great hero to me," he explained at the movie's premiere. "He's the *king* of all rock stars."

Okay, but what about Pepé Le Pew?

"Well, I've just always liked him."

Depp also reveals that Captain Jack's stagger wasn't necessarily caused by too much rum. It occurred to him that pirates would have to spend a lot of time in the hot sun of the Caribbean — obviously without air conditioning.

"So I would go into the sauna for great lengths of time," to see how it felt to be overheated, he told Oprah Winfrey, "which I don't recommend, by the way. You start to get a little woozy after about thirty minutes." He figured Captain Jack would be lightheaded half the time from the relentless heat.

In the end, Disney was wise to trust Depp. It was his utterly unexpected portrayal of Jack Sparrow that helped make the movie into 2003's most surprising blockbuster. The film would earn over $650 million worldwide and make Depp the unlikeliest of Hollywood action heroes. With a

Johnny Depp as Captain Jack Sparrow and Orlando Bloom as Will Turner in Pirates of the Caribbean: Curse of the Black Pearl. *The* Pirates *movies made Depp one of Hollywood's highest paid actors. "There are necessary evils. Money is an important thing in terms of representing freedom in our world. . . . You use your money to buy privacy because during most of your life you aren't allowed to be normal."*

salary of $20 million for each of the *Pirate* sequels, it also made him one of the highest paid.

Ironically, Johnny Depp wasn't the first actor considered for the movie. He wasn't even among the first half dozen—in part because nobody thought Depp would be interested in making a family film for Disney. But he has made a career out of doing the unexpected, of not following the traditional road to stardom, of living on his own terms.

"He always brings something different to everything he does," Verbinski commented to *People*. "There's no [baloney], no attitude. He enjoys acting and it shows."

He also fell into it by complete accident.

Unsettled

Johnny Depp's earliest memory is of catching lightning bugs. "And there was a little girl who lived next door who had a brace on her leg. We used to play on the swingset, and the night the astronauts landed on the moon, her father came out and looked up and said, in all seriousness, 'When man sets foot on the face of the moon, the moon will turn to blood,' " he recalled to writer Kevin Cook. "I stayed up watching the moon. It was a big relief when it didn't change."

While the moon may have stayed constant, little else in Depp's childhood would.

John Christopher Depp II was born in Owensboro, Kentucky, on June 9, 1963, the youngest of four siblings. His dad was a city engineer and his mom, Betty Sue, worked as a coffeeshop waitress. In 1970, John Sr. moved his family to Miramar, Florida.

"We moved like gypsies," Depp told Kevin Cook. "From the time I was five until my teens we lived in thirty or forty different houses. . . . But it's how I was raised so I thought there was nothing abnormal about it. Wherever the family is, that's home. We lived in apartments, on a farm, in a motel. Then we rented a house, and one night we moved from there to the house next door. I remember carrying my clothes across the yard and thinking, 'This is weird, but it's an easy move.' "

Growing up, Johnny assumed all families were like his—constantly moving from house to house with parents who constantly argued. "For a great number of years, my parents' relationship was very, very rocky," he said in an interview with *Playboy*. "That little kid who needs a strong foundation, a sense of security, safety . . . there were a number of years where I don't remember having that. I felt loved, but I also felt hated."

Growing up, Johnny assumed all families were like his—constantly moving from house to house with parents who constantly argued.

He recalled the time he was invited to dinner at his friend Sal Jenco's house. "It was like walking on Mars for the first time. . . . I found the fact that they ate salad before they had dinner was strange. Everybody sat down to dinner at a certain time. It was a completely different world. It was calm."

His parents finally divorced when he was fifteen. "It had been coming for quite a long time. I'm surprised they lasted that long, bless their hearts. I think they tried to keep it together for the kids, and then they couldn't anymore."

Depp admits it was still traumatic. "You just deal with it, but there's no escaping the hurt. I mean, it definitely hurts,

Despite earning the label as a rebel in his youth, Depp is very much a family man. He remains close to his mother, Betty Sue Palmer (left), and has two children with longtime partner, Vanessa Paradis (right). "There are four questions of value in life . . . ," he says. "What is sacred? Of what is the spirit made? What is worth living for, and what is worth dying for? The answer to each is the same. Only love."

man," he said in *US* magazine. "When my parents split up was when I think I realized . . . family is the most important thing in the world."

He was, and remains, especially close to his mom, calling her his best friend. "She's the greatest lady in the whole world; just unbelievable."

By the time his parents split, Johnny was seen by many as a borderline juvenile delinquent. He started smoking when he was eleven; lost his virginity when he was thirteen; ran with a pack of teens who amused themselves with vandalism and stealing, and eventually experimented with drugs. Even so, Johnny takes offense at the *bad boy* label.

He was, and remains, especially close to his mom, calling her his best friend. "She's the greatest lady in the whole world; just unbelievable."

"To me, it was much more curiosity," he explained to Steve Pond. "It wasn't like I was some malicious kid who wanted to kick an old lady in the shin and run. I just wanted to find out what was out there."

One thing Depp didn't like was bullies. As a kid, he had been taunted by classmates making fun of his name—Johnny Dip, Deppity Dog, Dippity-Do—so whenever his friends picked on anyone, "It got me so angry that I'd be on the poor guy's side," he told Cook.

The most important influence in his youth was music. "My first guitar was a real cheap little electric thing my mom bought me for twenty-five bucks when I was twelve," he said in a *Rolling Stone* interview. "From then on I don't remember puberty, I was just playing guitar."

Depp's father, John Sr., watches during his son's hand and footprint ceremony at Grauman's Chinese Theatre in Hollywood. John Depp Sr. was a civil engineer who moved his family over thirty times during Johnny's childhood.

Depp says he taught himself how to play by listening to records, then started playing in some garage bands. "The first group I was ever in was called Flame," he said in *Interview* magazine. "Then I was in The Kids." As his interest in music deepened, so did his disinterest in school. "I was in my third year of high school, and I didn't want to be there, and I was bored out of my mind, and I hated it. Teachers all thought I was going to end up in jail, a drug addict."

He later told the *Los Angeles Times*, "I wanted to play music so I kept doing that."

And within the year he'd be on the road with The Kids.

Reluctant Teen Idol

Although he'd later call himself a dumbass for dropping out of school, he explained to journalist Mark Bin, "The music was so important to me, I felt a sanctuary in it, a real safety, and in school, I didn't."

Dressed in crushed-velvet shirts he had borrowed from his mother, Johnny and his band played at clubs throughout Florida. "I was underage, but they would let me come in the back door to play," Depp recalled in *Interview*. "And then I'd have to leave after the first set. That's how I made a living."

He says the band's sound was a cross between U2 and the punk band The Clash. Over the next several years they played with a few big-name acts, including the Pretenders, the Ramones, and R.E.M. In 1983, Depp married makeup artist Lori Allison, and soon after, The Kids headed to Los Angeles in search of a record deal.

In Florida, The Kids had been considered fresh and original. In Los Angeles, they joined thousands of other bands trying to get noticed. With the competition so fierce, even club gigs were hard to come by. Johnny went to work at

Depp and his old band, The Kids, reunited to play at a January 2007 benefit concert dedicated to the memory of Sheila Witkin. Witkin was a longtime volunteer at the Neil Bogart Memorial Fund, raising money to combat pediatric cancers and AIDS.

a telemarketing company. "I sold fake grandfather clocks by phone for commissions," he told *Cosmopolitan*. "Horrible."

His marriage to Lori quickly fell apart and they separated, their divorce becoming final in early 1986. However, they stayed in touch, and she later introduced him to her new boyfriend, a young actor named Nicolas Cage— whose uncle was Academy Award–winning director Francis Ford Coppola. They became close friends, and one day Cage suggested that Depp meet his agent, Ilene Feldman.

"He came in with long hair and an earring and a T-shirt with cigarettes rolled up in the sleeve," Feldman recalled in

US. "He was not what someone usually looks like when they're coming in to look for an agent, which is what was so great about him: He just wasn't into it."

Feldman sent Johnny on an audition for a bit part in a new horror film, *A Nightmare on Elm Street.* The director, Wes Craven, had been looking for a blond surfer type but said Johnny "really had . . . that quiet charisma that none of the other actors had."

When he found out he got the job, Depp saw it as an easy way to make enough money in order to keep playing music. But the other Kids were angry. While he was doing the movie, the band broke up, so Johnny kept going on auditions and kept getting jobs.

"It was really just a way to pay the bills until the band and I got back together, or I got another band," he said in *Rolling Stone.* "Then there was a point, maybe a couple of years in, when I said, 'You know what? It seems like acting is the avenue I'm going down, so I should probably investigate what it's all about.' "

> Depp said, "You know what? It seems like acting is the avenue I'm going down, so I should probably investigate what it's all about."

It was at that point that his agent called with an audition for a new television series on the newly formed FOX network. "I said, 'No, no, no, no, no.' I didn't want to sign some big contract that would bind me for years," he recalled in *Interview.* It wasn't TV he objected to; it was the thought of being tied down.

Another actor was hired, then fired, a month into filming. The producers called Johnny's agent again, who urged him to take the job. After being told the average lifespan of a new

Twenty-one Jump Street turned Depp into an overnight TV teen idol, but his reluctance to being a "star" also earned him a reputation as being difficult. "They stick you with those names, those labels — rebel or whatever they like to use. Because they need a label; they need a name. They need something to put the price tag on the back of. . . . I am doing things that are true to me. The only thing I have a problem with is being labeled."

TV series is less than a full season, Depp finally agreed to read the script, which was about a cop who goes undercover at a high school as a guidance counselor. He liked the premise, "So I said okay."

Twenty-one Jump Street would become one of FOX network's first hit series and would be on the air for four years. It also made Depp Hollywood's newest heartthrob. He received over 10,000 fan letters a week, and his picture was plastered on the cover of every teen magazine.

And he hated everything about it.

An Actor's Actor

*A*lthough it frustrated him to be seen as a sex symbol, in the beginning Depp was pleased at the issues being tackled by *21 Jump Street*, such as safe sex, drugs, and molestation. As he told *TV Guide,* "What I thought when I originally started the show was, if I'm going to do a television series, I want to do something that means something."

He told Steve Pond that trying to help kids was why he spoke openly about his youth. "Hopefully, people can learn from it. Kids can say, 'Jesus, he went through the same thing I'm going through now. Maybe I'm not a bad kid like everybody says.' "

But by the third season, Depp felt the producers were more interested in marketing him on lunchboxes than in the quality of the show. By the time his contract was up in 1991, he was clearly eager to move on. When asked by a *Los Angeles Times* reporter if he'd consider another series, Depp adamantly said, "Never. I'd rather pump gas. I would never do it again, ever. There's not enough money in Los Angeles."

Johnny later acknowledged in the *New York Times,* "The series was great training, to work in front of a camera five days a week for four years. And it seems to have put me on the map, put me in a position to do things I really wanted to do." On the other hand, he noted, "It was never anything morally I felt comfortable with."

> *What Depp wanted was, he said, "To be good at what I do. To keep my integrity. To be happy."*

Even though Depp wasn't driven by a desire to be rich, he admitted to the *Los Angeles Times* that it was sometimes hard not to be tempted. "The money they offer you to do things that are, some of them, abysmal . . . there is really a devil on the one side, the angel on the other. Right now, the angel is winning."

While he appreciated what money could buy—such as a new house for his mom and step-dad, he told *Rolling Stone*'s Bill Zehme that "making a lot of money in this business didn't make me happy, so it's not my goal. It's now my turn to make choices and usually things I like are not commercials; not money-makers." What he wanted was, he said, "To be good at what I do. To keep my integrity. To be happy."

His first movie after the series ended, *Edward Scissorhands*, made him very happy. In the film, Edward is a Frankenstein-like creature who was given scissors for hands. Unable to touch anyone he cares for without slicing them, Edward is alone and isolated, until he is befriended by a young woman.

"It wasn't similar to anything I'd played before, to put it mildly," he told the *New York Times.* "Then I realized that Edward was all alone, and inside of all of us is this lonely

Depp costarred in Edward Scissorhands *with then-girlfriend Winona Ryder. "If there's any message to my work, it is ultimately that it's okay to be different, that it's good to be different, that we should question ourselves before we pass judgment on someone who looks different, behaves different, talks different, is a different color."*

little kid. Edward is a total outsider. I really know how that feels."

In real life, however, Johnny was anything but lonely. He was happily engaged and madly in love with his nineteen-year-old *Edward Scissorhands* costar Winona Ryder. They started dating in late 1989. Five months after their first date, Depp proposed.

Although Johnny swore Winona was the love of his life, others weren't so sure. Since divorcing Lori, he had also been engaged to actresses Sherilyn Fenn and Jennifer Grey.

Depp is always looking for creative challenges, admitting, "There's a drive in me that won't allow me to do certain things that are easy." In What's Eating Gilbert Grape, *Depp's character is torn between wanting to build a life with Becky (Juliette Lewis, right), and caring for his mentally handicapped brother, played by a young Leonardo DiCaprio (left).*

"When you're growing up, you go through a series of misjudgments," he explained in the *Los Angeles Times.* "Not bad choices, but wrong choices. I don't know what it is; possibly I was trying to rectify my family's situation or I was just madly in love." But, he stressed, "There's been nothing ever throughout my twenty-seven years that's comparable to the feeling I have with Winona." To prove it, he had *Winona Forever* tattooed on his right shoulder.

For the next two years, Johnny worked constantly, starring in *Benny & Joon; What's Eating Gilbert Grape?;* and another Tim Burton movie, *Ed Wood.* Each role was different from the last, and Depp was earning a reputation as one of Hollywood best, and most versatile, actors.

In Benny & Joon, *costarring Mary Stuart Masterson, Depp plays an illiterate. "With any part you play, there is a certain amount of yourself in it. There has to be, otherwise it's just not acting. It's lying." Part of his affinity for off-beat characters stems from the insecurity he suffered as a teenager. "I was the type of guy that never fitted in because he never dared to choose. I was convinced I had absolutely no talent at all. For nothing. And that thought took away all my ambition too."*

But his personal life unraveled. In 1993, Ryder ended their engagement, sending him into a lengthy depression. A volatile four-year relationship with Kate Moss ended in 1998. Depp was drinking too much, which led to angry outbursts. He wondered out loud in the press if he'd ever find someone to settle down with and start a family.

He would.

The Sexiest Man Alive Settles Down

*I*n 1998, Depp was in Paris filming a supernatural horror film called *The Ninth Gate.* He was in the lobby of the Hotel Costes when he saw a woman facing away from him. Her dress exposed her back, and Johnny tried to explain to writer Eric Hadegaard the affect it had on him.

"Whammo, man, across the room, amazing, incredible, awesome."

The woman was French actress/singer Vanessa Paradis, whom Depp had met in passing several years earlier. When she saw him, Vanessa walked over to say hello. Johnny joked in *Vanity Fair,* "I knew at that moment when she came up to me, I was ruined."

Within a few months, Paradis was pregnant and the couple had moved in together in the south of France. Their daughter Lily-Rose was born on May 27, 1999. A son, Jack, would follow three years later. Having kids was a life-changing experience for Depp.

He admitted to *Newsweek's* Sean Smith that at times during his career, "I had these sort of self-destructive periods," because he was angry at the paparazzi, angry at losing his privacy. "I couldn't get a grasp on it, so I spent years poisoning myself. I was very, very good at it. But when my daughter was born, suddenly . . . I wasn't angry anymore. It was like a veil being lifted. Looking back on it now, it was simply a waste of time, all that self-medicating and boozing.

"Finally I was faced with a critical decision: Do I want to continue to be a dumbass or do I want not to be a dumbass?"

He did not, so he stopped. Depp gave up hard liquor and now limits himself to a couple glasses of wine. He has even cut back significantly on cigarettes. Director Tim Burton, with whom Depp has made six pictures, including *Charlie and the Chocolate Factory, Corpse Bride,* and 2007's *Sweeney Todd,*

Depp plays Willy Wonka in Tim Burton's 2005 remake of Charlie and the Chocolate Factory. *Burton believes fatherhood has made Johnny a better actor. Depp knows it's made him a more fulfilled person. "I never in my life thought it was possible to feel such deep love, such an incredible connection. . . . It's all kinds of these profound things crashing on you when your child arrives into the world. It's like you've met your reason to live."*

observed that being a father "released him from the pressure of finding meaning and identity exclusively in his work. I think it softened him on one level, and then invigorated him on an artistic one."

Johnny agrees. "Now I know where home is. For me, family is the most important thing in the world." When his young daughter was hospitalized in March 2007 with an E. coli virus infection, he immediately left the set of *Sweeney Todd* and rushed back home. He stayed by Lily's side until doctors assured him she was out of danger.

> *After spending so many years doing small and independent films, Johnny was in the year's biggest hit.*

Depp also gives his time and money to help other kids. He's been honored by the Los Angeles Children's Hospital for his generous donations, and he is active with War Child, an organization that helps children around the world who are affected by war.

Although he continued to select the films he found most interesting or challenging, as his children got older, Depp admits he started thinking it would be fun to star in a movie they could see. While meeting with a Disney executive, Johnny mentioned how much he'd enjoy providing a voice for a character in one of their animated films. Instead, he was offered a role in *Pirates of the Caribbean.* Johnny agreed on the spot.

When the movie was announced, many critics thought it was a terrible idea and predicted the film would flop. So did most Disney executives. It didn't. After spending so many

Depp was honored by L.A.'s Children's Hospital for his charitable contributions. The success of Pirates *has enabled him to both help others and adopt a more relaxed outlook on life. "I think the thing to do is to enjoy the ride while you're on it. . . . Life's pretty good, and why wouldn't it be? I'm a pirate, after all."*

years doing small and independent films, Johnny was in the year's biggest hit. It also earned him his first Oscar nomination for Best Actor. The *Pirates* sequel, *Dead Man's Chest*, was even more successful, becoming only the third film in history to earn over $1 billion worldwide.

The third *Pirates* movie, *At World's End*, was released May 25, 2007, and broke the record for best Memorial Day Weekend debut, earning over $140 million.

"You feel like you have infiltrated the enemy camp," he said to *Rolling Stone*. "Like you got in there somehow and chiseled your name in the castle wall. It just felt right. Even now, with the dolls and the cereal boxes and snacks and fruit juices, it all just feels fun to me."

Pirates of the Caribbean: At World's End *was released May 25, 2007, completing the* Pirates *trilogy. Characters in the movie are, from left to right: Captain Barbossa (Geoffrey Rush), Will Turner (Orlando Bloom), Captain Jack Sparrow (Johnny Depp), Elizabeth Swann (Keira Knightley), and Captain Sao Feng (Yun-Fat Chow).*

    The success of the films allowed Depp to fulfill a long-held dream. In late 2004 he bought his own thirty-five-acre island in the Bahamas for $3 million. Named Little Hall's Pond Cay, it's a mile long and a little over 440 yards wide. It has two cottages, six white sand beaches, and a lagoon. For Johnny, it's the perfect place to go and do absolutely nothing in between film roles and playing music with various bands.

    Looking back at his life, Depp told *Newsweek,* "I think everything happened the way it was meant to happen, but I don't know why. But this is where I am. So I enjoy it, salute it and keep moving forward."

1963	John Christopher Depp II is born in Owensboro, Kentucky, on June 9.
1975	He gets first guitar.
1978	Johnny's parents divorce.
1980	He drops out of high school to pursue a music career.
1983	He and his band, the Kids, move to Los Angeles. He marries makeup artist Lori Allison.
1984	He starts going on acting auditions. Separates from Lori. At the urging of Nicolas Cage, Johnny auditions for a movie. His first film, *A Nightmare on Elm Street,* opens November 16.
1986	Johnny and Lori Allison's divorce is final. He begins a two-year relationship with actress Sherilyn Fenn.
1987	He is cast in *21 Jump Street.*
1990	Announces engagement to Winona Ryder in February; leaves TV series in July.
1993	Engagement to Ryder ends in June; becomes co-owner of The Central nightclub, which will eventually be called The Viper Room.
1994	Starts dating Kate Moss in January.
1995	*P,* the album by his band P, is released.
1997	Makes directorial debut on *The Brave.*
1998	Begins relationship with French actress/singer Vanessa Paradis
1999	Vanessa gives birth to their first child, Lily-Rose Melody Depp, on May 27.
2002	Their son Jack John Christopher Depp III is born on April 9.
2003	*Pirates of the Caribbean: The Curse of the Black Pearl* opens July 9. It eventually earns over $1 billion worldwide.
2004	Depp is nominated for a Best Actor Oscar for his portrayal of Captain Jack. He buys an island in the Bahamas.
2006	*Pirates of the Caribbean: Dead Man's Chest* opens July 7.
2007	Depp wins three People's Choice Awards in January; *Pirates of the Caribbean: At World's End* opens May 25.

FILMOGRAPHY

2008	*The Rum Diary*
	Shantaram
2007	*Sweeney Todd*
	Pirates of the Caribbean: At World's End
	Joe Strummer: The Future is Unwritten (documentary)
2006	*Pirates of the Caribbean: Dead Man's Chest*
	Deep Sea 3D (narrator/documentary)
2005	*Charlie and the Chocolate Factory*
	Corpse Bride
2004	*Finding Neverland*
	Secret Window
	The Libertine
	Happily Ever After
	King of the Hill (Voice/TV series)
2003	*Breakfast with Hunter*
	Once Upon a Time in Mexico
	Charlie: The Life and Art of Charles Chaplin
	Pirates of the Caribbean: The Curse of the Black Pearl
2002	*Lost in La Mancha* (documentary)
2001	*From Hell*
	Blow
2000	*Before Night Falls*
	Chocolat
	The Man Who Cried
1999	*The Source* (documentary)
	Sleepy Hollow
	The Ninth Gate
	The Astronaut's Wife

1998	*Fear and Loathing in Las Vegas*
	Top Secret (narrator/TV documentary)
	L.A. Without a Map
1997	*The Brave*
	Donnie Brasco
1996	*Cannes Man*
1995	*Dead Man*
	Nick of Time
	Don Juan DeMarco
1994	*Ed Wood*
1993	*What's Eating Gilbert Grape?*
	Benny & Joon
	Arizona Dream
1991	*Freddy's Dead: The Final Nightmare*
1990	*Cry-Baby*
	Edward Scissorhands
1987– 1991	*21 Jump Street* (TV series)
1987	*Hotel* (TV series guest spot)
1986	*Platoon*
	Slow Burn (TV movie)
1985	*Private Resort*
	Lady Blue (TV series guest spot)
1984	*A Nightmare on Elm Street*

Other

2008	*Shantaram* (Producer)
2008	*The Rum Diary* (Writer and Director)
1997	*The Brave* (Executive Producer)

Books

Johnstone, Nick. *Johnny Depp: The Illustrated Biography.* London: Carlton Publishing, 2006.

Goodall, Nigel. *Johnny Depp: The Biography.* London: John Blake Publishing, 1999.

Robb, Brian. *Johnny Depp: A Modern Rebel.* Medford, NJ: Plexus Publishing, 2006.

Works Consulted

Binelli, Mark. "The Last Buccaneer." *Rolling Stone,* March 1, 2007. http://www.rollingstone.com/news/story/10714717/the_last_buccaneer

Burke, Tom. "Hollywood's Tough, Rough New Romeo." *Cosmopolitan,* January 1991.

Caron, Isabelle. *Hello Magazine.* July 29, 2003. http://www.johnnydeppfan.com/interviews/hello03.htm

Collins, Glenn. "Johnny Depp Contemplates Life As, and After, *Scissorhands.*" *New York Times,* 1991.

Cook, Kevin. "Playboy Interview: Johnny Depp." *Playboy,* January 1996.

Daly, Steven. "The Maverick King." *Vanity Fair,* November 2004.

Hedegaard, Erik. "Johnny Darko." *Rolling Stone.* February 10, 2005.

Keck, William. "A Window into His Soul." *Los Angeles Times,* April 1, 2001.

The Late Show with David Letterman, July 27, 2006. http://www.thetubevideo.com/2006/07/31/the-late-show-with-david-letterman-johnny-depp/

Offman, Craig. "Johnny Depp Battles Editor over Comma." Salon.com, July 22, 1999. http://www.salon.com/books/log/1999/07/22/depp/index.html

Pond, Steve. "Depp Perception." *US,* June 26, 1989.

Schneller, Johanna. "Johnny Depp: Girls' Best Friend." *Rolling Stone,* December 1998.

Smith, Sean. "Pirate's Life." *Newsweek,* June 26, 2006.

Warren, Elaine. "Bad Boy to Role Model." *TV Guide,* January 23, 1988.

Waters, John. "Johnny Depp." *Interview,* April 1990.

Willman, Chris. "From Baby Face to 'Cry-Baby.' " *Los Angeles Times,* April 4, 1990.

Zehme, Bill. "Sweet Sensation." *Rolling Stone,* January 10, 1991.

Web Addresses

The Johnny Depp Zone
http://www.johnnydepp-zone.com/deppster/

Fan Page for Johnny Depp—Interviews
http://www.johnnydeppfan.com/interviews/interviews.htm

INDEX